Books written

The Outlaw and His Family

Continuance

Love Heals

LOVE HEALS

The Outlaw and His Family

JUDY INGRAM

WESTBOW
PRESS®
A DIVISION OF THOMAS NELSON
& ZONDERVAN

WestBow Press books may be ordered through booksellers or by contacting:

WestBow Press
A Division of Thomas Nelson & Zondervan
1663 Liberty Drive
Bloomington, IN 47403
www.westbowpress.com
1 (866) 928-1240

ISBN: 978-1-9736-1240-7 (sc)
ISBN: 978-1-9736-1239-1 (e)

Print information available on the last page.

WestBow Press rev. date: 12/22/2017

Gloria had been broken about her husband, Frank, and the way that he had treated her. He had seemed to love her at the time that they had married. When he joined the church where she was a member, he was very kind and caring. These thoughts ran through Gloria's mind during the week-end when she and her son, Bobby were waiting for Monday to start to work at Russel's Merchantile Store.

Thank God that things were working out for her and her son, Bobby. She did not want to reminise about Frank but the hurt had been too great to get over in such a short time. She thought that the scars would last forever. A few years after Bobby was born, Frank became a different man. He started cursing at her and she wondered what she had done to cause his reactions toward her. She was fine during the day when Frank was in the fields working. But when he came home she walked on pins and needles; afraid to say anything that might set him off. Her life was about Frank, she had always put her desires second to his. She always kept the house clean, his clothes washed and his meals cooked on time. He became very demanding. Sometimes she felt like his slave and not a wife. After Frank's father died he got a little worse every year. The farm that his father owned was in foreclosure. Frank did not know that his father had misused his money and did not pay the mortgage during the past year. Frank believed that the farm would be his after his father died.

Frank was in shock, he did not have the money to pay for the farm. What was he suppose to do now?

Mr. Mosley bought the farm that Frank had grown up on. Frank had worked the farm all of his life. Mr. Mosley allowed Frank to be his tenant farmer. Frank did not talk to Gloria about his feelings or what had happened. He just bottled all of his feelings up inside and put all of his energy into working. When Gloria questioned him about his changed life, Frank just blew up and yelled at Gloria. When it came time for Frank to release his feelings, Gloria and Bobby were in his way. The time came when Frank no longer just yelled at Gloria, he would also strike her with his hand. Bobby was old enough that he knew when his ma got hurt. It hurt Bobby to see his dad physically abuse his ma. But he was small and could do nothing about it. When Bobby did say something about his pa hurting his ma, Frank just took Bobby by the arm and threw him on the couch. Then he would walk out and slam the door behind him.

Each year the yellings and hittings got more intense. Gloria never entertained friends. She always stayed home and tried everything to keep the peace. She tried to protect Bobby as much as she could. Gloria prayed and prayed for Frank's relationship with the Lord. The Lord she grew up loving and serving; Praying that Frank would turn around.

A friend of the family stopped by one day to see if Bobby could play with his son. When Frank saw his friend talking with Gloria at the front door, he became outraged. Jealously boiled over him. Frank walked up to the man and hit him hard. The man tried to explain but Frank would not hear any of it. The man left in a hurry and Frank pulled Gloria into the house. He threw her against the wall. Gloria was pregnant with their second child. She lost the baby the next day. What could she do, she had no where to go. She had lived a sheltered life with no close friends. As she suffered she tried to carry on as if nothing had happened. Frank had no compassion for her. Bobby had tried to stop him but he just made it much worse by trying to help his mother. After Bobby's twelfth birthay and finishing the sixth grade in school, he decided to run away thinking that it would help his ma by staying out of the way. *Maybe if I were not around, pa would be easier on ma*, he thought. He had only the clothes that he was wearing. He kept walking until he came to a town fifty miles away. He thought no one would find him, he was so far from home. That is when he saw a cafe and waited behind the building to see if anyone would throw away the garbage. He did not want to beg, not yet anyway. He would try to find a job. He walked down the street and found an open church house. He figured that he could spend the night there. One day Katie saw Bobby hiding behind her cafe and started putting some extra food in a bag to leave for him to find.

One morning when Luke was waiting for Nancy to walk her to school, he saw a boy walking from the church. That night Luke saw the same boy go into the church. Early the next morning, Luke sought after the boy. When they met, they became friends. Luke's dad, the pastor, and the sheriff helped Bobby and his mother reunite. Bobby's dad was dead; Killed by the horse that he had been beating. Gloria needed to put the past behind her now and move on. She and Bobby would start to work Monday at the merchantile store. Ross Russell had hired them to help him since his store was expanding in business.

Working for Ross was a pleasure. He was very nice and generous to Bobby and Gloria. Gloria would never trust another man as long as she lived. Her hurts had been too strong. Thank God that she did feel free to worship Him as she should. No one in town knew Gloria's situation, except that her husband had been killed in an accident. Pastor Joe and the sheriff knew of her situation because they had been the ones to help her and her son.

Gloria and Bobby had been working for more than three months now. They were enjoying their new home and they were beginning to make new friends. They had even joined County Church. Gloria became very efficient at the cash register. She cleaned and dusted during customer lax time. Gloria also fixed up beautiful displays in the window. The displays attracted customers and the business grew even more. Ross had given her a raise in salary and was amazed at her attributes. She surely was an asset for the company. Bobby did very well stocking and counting inventory. He caught on his job very fast and learned all of the trade. Ross had taught him well.

Gloria was a very good sales person. Whenever a lady came to buy material, Gloria helped her select the material that would look the best on the buyer. Women were shopping just for Gloria's expertise. The business came natural to her and she was enjoying it.

Sometimes Ross would buy dinner for Gloria and Bobby and they would set in the kitchen back of the store area and have dinner together. The small kithchen had a square table with four chairs. The kitchen had a pump and sink by the back window. Ross was thinking about putting electricity in the store. They would talk about the store and what needed to be purchased. Bobby knew what buyers wanted mostly and would order bigger supplies. He knew how to meet the needs of his customers. Ross was very pleased with his help. The town was beginning to become more modern and Ross had to keep up with the times.

A couple of weeks later Ross had electricity insalled in his business. He installed electricity in his apartment on the second floor and also Gloria's apartment in the new addition.

"Ross, these electric lights are wonderful. What a marvelous invention. I am glad to be living in a time of eletricity. So many new things are being invented. I wonder what will be next?" asked Gloria.

"I hope someone will invent something that will make travel much faster," said Ross. "These order shipments just can't get here fast enough. Most people wanted their order yesterday. I will just have to take one day at the time and wait on progress. I am happy that the train fianlly made it here."

Lizzy came into the store to buy clothing materials for her family. "Good morning, Gloria, I need your expertize for a lady that I recently met. I was wondering if you could help me. She is about the same size as you. I do believe that she would look very pretty in this teal color. But I need accessories to match this lovely color. What do you suggest?"

"Teal is a very lovely color. A cream color would go well, not too bright and not too dull. What do you think?"

"That does sound lovely. I will put it to the test. I see just the right hat that will match." Gloria agreed and Lizzy bought the material and hat with other materials. Lizzy never let on that she, Lydia, D'Anna, Claire, and Abby were making a dress for Gloria.

On the way home, Lizzy stopped at Abby's to say hello and let her know when the next sewing session would be. Rae had purchased a new sewing maching for her and she was ready to try it out. The ladies in her family would love it and purchase one for themselves. Abby met Lizzy at the door.

"I thought I saw you down the street. Please come in and have tea with me. Gin took the children shopping and I am all yours."

"Abby, I am calling on our sisters for another sewing session. I have a surprise for all of you. I want to tell and show you all at the same time. Can you come tomorrow?"

"I will be there and bring my materials too. Maybe we can desisgn some new fashions. I love when we get together to sew and discuss fashions. I was talking with Mr. Russell at the merchantile store and he said that Gloria wanted to set up a special dress section for the ladies. Mr. Russell has already ordered the racks. Gloria does not have time to sew. She works six days a week. She only has a couple of hours in the evening to make clothes," siad Abby.

"You amaze me, Abby, you just read my mind. I bought material for Gloria thinking that we could make her a new dress. We will discuss all this tomorrow at the sewing. I need to go, I will look forward to seeing you tomorrow." Lizzy left smiling thinking about how the sisters all seemed to have the same thoughts of the mind.

After Lizzy left Abby's, she drove her buggy over to Ryon' s and Claire's farm. She saw Claire by the rose garden. "Claire will you be able to come over tomorrow for a sewing session? All of the ladies are getting together. I believe it is time for us to put our minds together and come up with something new."

"That will be wonderful. I will ask our cook, Janice Jones if she will baby-sit Theresa for me. If you are making rounds to all of us it will take you all day."

"I am enjoying spending the day visiting the family. Except for Lorisa, that will take almost two days to see her. I will write her and fill her in on our plans. Maybe we should think about giving our group a name. Our very own special name."

"That sounds interesting, I will be thinking about that. You had better hurry so that you can get home before dark. When you see D'Anna, tell her hello for me."

Lizzy made her way over to the Ingram's ranch, her mind going one hundred miles per hour. She had a lot to think about and she was excited. When Lizzy reached the ranch she saw John working by the stables. "Hello John, is D'Anna home?"

"D'Anna and Lydia, both are in the house. Just go right on in."

Lizzy walked in the front door and called out D'Anna's name. "We are in the sewing room, come on in." D'Anna went to meet Lizzy in the front room. "What a nice surprise, what brings you here this late? It is good to see you." They walked into the sewing room and sat down.

"Lydia and I are making bed sheets for the bunk house. We are just about finished. Work is never ending but I am glad to be working."

"I just came by to invite you two to a sewing session tomorrow at my house. I have a few plans in mind and would like for us all to get together and see what we can come up with. I can not stay. It is getting late and I want to get home before dark. Willy and Lilly will be hungry after a long day at school. So will I see y'all tomorrow?"

"We will be there with bells on," said Lydia. "I love new ideas. What did you have in mind?"

"For one thing, I would like for us to give ourselves and our projects a name. Be thinking it over and we can discuss it tomorrow. I need to run. See Y'all tomorrow. I will see myself out."

The next day, Lydia, D'Anna, Abby, and Claire met a Lizzy's home. The sewing room was getting a little crowded with all the sisters and sisters-in-law. It was a good thing that Rae had extended the rooms in the house and added bigger ones. "Okay ladies, now that we are all here together, I want to show you my brand new sewing machine that Rae bought me for my birthday." Lizzy uncovered her sewing machine and everyone started investigating it.

"It is a fine looking machine," said Abby. "Now sit down at it and show us how it works."

Lizzy demonstrated the sewing machine method to them and it whizzed like a charm. "It is so fast. It cuts out half of my sewing time. I can make more clothes than ever and I have more time to spend with my family. I just love it. What do you all think?"

"The first thing that I am going to do when I get home is talk to John. Why hadn't Rae mentioned it to him. Guess it was just too soon."

"Mr. Russell will be ordering quite a few of theses now that we have all seen it. I can hardly wait to get mine," mentioned Claire.

Everyone took out their materials and started designing new pieces and asking each other what they thought. "Ladies we need a name for ourselves, our sewing sessions and our projects. Does anyone have any suggestions?" asked Lizzy. "Remember that this name will go before our dress space at the merchantile."

"Now that is another subject," said Claire. "You mean that we will make many dresses and children's clothes and Gloria will display them for us? Mr. Russell does let us sell a few pieces of clothes already, but this will be even better. Gloria is doing a fantastic job at the merchantile."

"She has given it a woman's touch and I am enjoying her displays. She really has a mind full of wonderful ideas. More women are shopping there everyday just for her opinion on certain items," said Lydia.

"We will talk to her and help her with the ladies apparel," said Abby. "Lizzy tell us all what you had in mind about Gloria's dress."

"Yes, Gloria works so much that she does not have hardly any time to sew at all. I picked up this beatiful teal material and thought that it would look fantastic on her. With our minds put together we can fashion this to suit her church wear. Isn't this color just lovely? It will go well with her dark, brown, aubourn hair and her lavender eyes."

"Do you have her measurements? I believe that she is about Lorisa's size. A little petite and most beautiful. She will have the men turning their heads. I truly pray that she likes it," said D'Anna." Everyone started working on the dress, extra dresses for women to wear, children's clothes and a few shirts for the men. They also made Bobby a couple of new shirts.

"Well, what names have you all thought about for ourselves?" asked Lizzy.

"We all do a lot of sewing and we sit in this same circle almost every time that we are here, so my choice is the *"The Sewing Circle,"* said D'Anna.

"Who is next?"

"We are all stitching and using our valuable time," said Abby. "I choose *A Stitch in Time.*

"How does *Made With Honor* sound?" said Lydia.

"You would use the work honor since you are married to a preacher," said Lizzy. "How does *A Splach with a Dash* sound? A few splashes of color and a few dashes of lines. You know that I am a little dramatic with these new styles."

"People give all kinds of names. We could lable it *"The Clothes Line,"* said Claire.

"Knowing Lorisa, she would want to name it after some kind of musical note," said Abby.

"Since we all have different names. Let us take a break, have tea and cookies, then come back to vote on the name. The one with the most votes wins. How does that sound?"

Each one said "Perfect" and took a break.

During the break, they could not help it, they all discussed the name for the sewing sessions. When the break was over and they all gathered back into the sewing room, Lizzy asked. "What did you all come up with? Should we have a silent vote?"

"It seems to me that we wanted something simple and just plain and meaningful. I will agree with D'Anna and vote *The Sewing Circle,*"said Abby.

"Okay that is two votes for *The Sewing Circle*. What does everyone else say?" said Lizzy.

"I also agree with with them, I like it too," said Claire.

"Count me in also," said Lydia.

"That settles it then. We are officially *The Sewing Circle*. Congratulatins to all of us. Now we have a name. This will be our label on all the clothes that we make. We need to talk with Gloria and let her know about our decisions. I am sure that she will be overjoyed with our line of clothes," said Lizzy.

3

A month later, Lizzy visited Gloria at the merchantile store and asked her if she would join her and her sisters Sunday afternoon at the ranch. Gloria agreed and made plans for the visit. "Bobby, Lizzy invited us to visit her and her sisters at Rae's ranch this Sunday after church. Would you like to come with me to the ranch?"

"Oh, mom, I meant to tell you that Ross and I are going fishing after church this Sunday. Guess that will work out for all of us."

Pastor Joe Hodges was preaching about jealousy that Sunday. The Bible mentions jealousy all through the Old and New Testament. Jealousy turns an attitude to strife. It tries to stop God's work. You become selfish and think only of your desires and wants. You think that you are better than someone else and it leads to spiritual pride. It says in 1 Samuel that jealousy starts as you resent a rival; you want to remove that person from your life. Get a hold of yourself and read what the Bible teaches about jealousy. Don't ruin your life by such a sin. God loves everyone the same. Look to that person and be happy for him or her. Jealousy can tear apart a friendship and lead you to think and do wrong things. Avoid jealousy by rejoicing in their success. Let God be in control of their life and in your life. He may have something better for you. So put it all into His hands and trust and obey Him. He wants a close relationship with you.

Each one of you is very special to Him. You have your own personal relationship with Him only. You are all a very unique individual. He made us all different for His purpose. Pastor Hodges continued on with a very meaningful lesson and the congregation took it to heart.

Lydia was enjoying being a pastor's wife. Joe's, son Luke and his daughter Nancy were Lydia's step children but she considered them hers. Helen, Joe's first wife, had been a good friend of hers. Helen had died carrying her unborn baby. No one knew about the baby except Joe and the doctor. Luke and Nancy were old enough that they could baby-sit for their two younger siblings, Joe Jr., and Grace. Lydia was John Ingram's sister, who had married D'Anna Jefferson and was considered a sister in the Jefferson family.

Gloria rode to the ranch with Rae, Lizzy, Willy, and Lilly Sunday afternoon after church. When they got home, The Sewing Circle and their families were already there.

"I am glad that you could come with us," said Lizzy. "Did Bobby have other plans?"

"Yes, he alraedy had made plans to go fishing with Ross for the afternoon."

"It looks like everyone is here. Aunt Jame and Uncle Eli are preparing the picnic table. A huge live oak tree shaded the table and the area around it. "I'll go see if I can help," said Rae.

Lizzy and the children went inside the house to put on play clothes. The ladies pitched in to help Aunt Jame and Uncle Eli, while the children started playing. The yard was filled with family. After dinner, the ladies gathered into the sewing room to talk with Gloria.

"Gloria we are very thankful for the expertise that you are expressing at the merchantile store. All of us sisters wanted to show our appreciation for you kindness and the help that you have shown us while we were shopping. We would like to present you with a dress that we all made and a couple of shirts for Bobby," said Lizzy.

D'Anna handed Gloria the dress and the two shirts in a folded package. "Go aheard and open it. We do pray that you like it, if not, let us know. We love working on new designs."

Gloria was very much surprised, "You all are just so kind." Gloria opened the package and took out the dress and held it up to her. "It is very beatiful. You are all magnificient seamtresses. I wish that I could sew this well. How can I ever repay such wonderful thoughtfulness. It seems to be a perfect fit. I will wear it next Sunday to church."

"We are happy that you like it," said Abby. "We know that you do not get much time to sew since you work six days a week. We all are glad that you are here and part of our church family."

"Now that we are all here together," said Claire. "We can discuss our dress section at the merchantile. Gloria you can tell us what you need and if you'd like we will help you arrange the racks and clothes."

"It just so happens that I talked with Ross about the clothes space and he is willing to let us have our very own room in the expanded building. We can set up a window display with mannequins and expose dresses for the ladies and shirts for the men. We can start as early as next week. I will clean a place and get it all ready. We can have our very own dress shop," said Gloria.

The afternoon flew by and the sun was beginning to set. "Gloria, would you mind if Joe and I take you home since we live down the street from you. Our buggy has room enough and that will save Lizzy a trip."

"That is fine with me. Thank all of you again for the dress and the shirts. I am sure that Bobby will be very thankful as I am. These are better than the magazine orders. You all have made me feel very welcome here. It has been almost eight months and I feel like I really belong here."

Rae, John, Mark, Joe, and Ryon helped clean up the picnic table and put the chairs back into the barn. As they were finishing putting away all of the dinner items, they heard the horses in the caral making erie noises.

Rae and John went over to find out what all the commotion was about. There to find a rattle snake close to the horses. Ryon had noticed, got the shot gun from the barn and headed over toward Rae and John. The men held the horses while Ryon shot the snake. "We need to be on the look-out more ofter for these critters, " said Ryon.

"Where there is one, there will be another," said John.

Joe came around, "all is well, thank God no one was bitten. I am glad that the children are safe in the kitchen having ice cream with Aunt Jame, Uncle Eli, and Ms Dillon."

"Ice cream sounds good to me," said Mark. "I believe that I will go join them."

"Let's all go," said Rae.

There were plenty of left overs after dinner so Rae and Lizzy packed up some plates to take to Carlos and Teresa. Rae knocked on Carlos's door. Carlos opened the door and greeted Rae. "Hello Rae, it is a pleasure for you to come visit."

"Carlos, my family just had a very large dinner. We had plenty of left overs and we wanted to share these plates with you and your family."

Lizzy had met Teresa outside with Jose and Rachel. "Hello Teresa, hello Jose and Rachel. You children are growing so very big. Soon I will not be able to recognize you two. Your flowers are beautiful. I especially love the yellow rose bushes. Teresa, we are overflowing with food. We hope that you will enjoy Aunt Jame and Uncle Eli's meals."

"Thank you very much Mrs. Eliza. Your thoughtfulness is very well appreciated. I'm sure that we all will enjoy this. You brought a whole pie. What kind is it. It must be apple. Only an apple pie can have a crust that looks that scrumptious."

"You guessed it right. It is apple and very delicious. The family has already eaten two. I was so full that I could not eat another bite. I hope you enjoy it. Aunt Jame and Uncle Eli just love to share their meals."

"We are grateful for that. I have eaten some of their meals and I could learn some lessons from them."

Rae was telling Carlos about the snake incident and told him to be on the loo-kout. "Rae, I found a puppy running around by the stream. No one has claimed her. I will take care of her until I hear that she belongs to someone else. She seems to be about seven months old. She has become part of our family. It will be hard to give her up. She has already alerted us about critters being in the yard and around the chicken pen. If you hear of anyone that has lost a dog, let me know."

"Carlos I am sure that the owner is glad that the dog is missing. From my experienced years out here, dogs have many puppies and the owner can not feed them all. They seem to be glad to lose a few puppies. But I will let you know just in case."

Rae called out to Lizzy. "Lizzy are you ready to go? Good day Carlos I will see you around."

Lizzy said good by to Teresa, Jose, and Rachel and they headed home.

4

The next day at work, Ross had ordered dinner for Gloria, Bobby, and himself. When the food arrived, Ross put a closed sign at the door that had "Out to dinner" written on it. Sometimes Ross made this extra time to give Gloria and Bobby a small break from work. "The food is here and we can retire into the kitchen and have dinner," said Ross smiling.

Gloria and Bobby followed Ross into the kitchen. "Ross this looks delicious and smell that aroma. You should not have gone to all this trouble."

Ross was beginning to fall in love with Gloria without her knowledge. He did not know how she would feel toward him since he was eight years older. He knew that she had a hard marriage and she paid no attention to the men that entered the store except to checking out their merchandise at the cash register, though she was very friendly. After the meal, Gloria began to clean up and Ross lightly placed his hand over hers. "I will get this if you would like to freshen up before going back to work," Ross commented.

Gloria slowly moved her hand and started throwing away the paper wrappings from the sandwiches. She felt the odd feeling of Ross'a touch. She did not know how to respond toward the gesture. She just ignored it and left to freshen up. She thought a lot of Ross but she was unable to trust another man. Ross had been a giving and wonderful employer to her and she admired him very much.

Ross felt a little embarressed and just started cleaning up the kitchen. He wanted to win Gloria's love but he wasn't sure how.

That next Sunday Gloria wore the beautiful teal dress to church. She, Bobby, and Ross walked to church together since Ross lived next door to her in his upstairs apartment above the merhantile. When Ross met her and Bobby outside to walk with them to church, he just staired and held his breath. She looked too pretty in her new dress and he noticed that Bobby was wearing a new shirt. He knew who the seamtresses were. He had sold many of their clothes. "Gloria, I can not help it, You look fantastic this morning. What a lovely dress. It befits you perfectly." Ross was beginning to feel a little jealous. He knew that Gloria would attract many looks. But he passed it over and was proud to escourt her to church.

When Gloria walked into the church, the men turned their heads to see Gloria. The women turned their heads too and thought how lovely she looked. They had never seen Gloria looking so stylish. When D'Anna saw her walk in with Ross she commented to John. "John, Gloria looks so very lovely this morning, doesn't she?'

"Yes she really does look pretty but you know the most beautiful woman in the world is sitting beside of me." D'Anna eyed John and just took his hand in hers.

Durning the service, Pastor Joe Hodges followed up his message about jealously and added a few words about how love heals a broken heart. "Love heals, but healing comes from God. Put your faith and trust in Him. No matter how much you have been hurt, the Bible teaches us to forgive, look to the future and move on for His sake. God is our ultimate healer and we must continue on for Him. Forget our past, we can do nothing about it. But we can do something about today, the present. Why let the past keep you full of unwanted hurt when you can have all the blessings that God has waiting for you. You will not find out what these blessings are if you continue in the past. It keeps you from serving the Lord as you should. Put all of your troubles into His hands and He will sustain you. Most of us have been there some time or the other. Only you can make the choice to move on and not dwell in the past. God has plans for all of you. Do you not want to know what they are? Let Him lead and guide you. Wait on Him to fill your life with joy. Remember the fruit of the Spirit in Galatians 5; love,joy, peace, patience, kindness, goodness, faithfulness, gentleness, and self control. Let us go home with these gifts from the Holy Spirit and be better people for Jesus."

Gloria was thinking in her heart and mind what Pastor Joe said. That is exactly what she wanted to do. She would make the choice to serve God and not the world by putting away her hurt feelings and feeling sorry for herself. She needed to go out and help others, not be a hindrance to them. She felt like a new person. She felt the freedom and she praised the Lord to be free. Bobby had told her that he had accepted the Lord as his personal saviour. She needed to talk to him about getting baptised.

When Ross walked Gloria and Bobby home, Gloria invided Ross to dinner. She had cooked it ahead of time and it was already ready, waiting to be eaten. "Ross, please come upstairs and have dinner with Bobby and me. I have not heard a lot about your fishing trip and you and Bobby can fill me in. Guess I have been too busy."

"How about that Bobby, are you gain to let your mom know all of our fishing secrets?"

"We don't have to tell her everything, do we?" asked Bobby.

At dinner, Ross said the blessings upon the food and the family. His words showed Gloria what kind of heart Ross had. She liked what she heard. Maybe she could become fond of another man afterall. But she would not let her guard down just yet.

Bobby broke into her thoughts. "Mom, you should have seen Ross catch that big bass and just as he was reeling it in; it got so close to his hand, then the line broke."

"That is okay Bobby, we will get him the next time," said Ross. "Bobby did quite well for himself. He decided to throw those three fish back into the stream. Guess he did not want to gut and clean them. Is that why you threw them back in, Bobby?"

"No, not really, they were so pretty that I did not have the heart to kill them. But, I am getting hungry for fish just talking about them. I will clean the next ones."

Dinner was over too fast. "Let me help you wash these dishes. The meal was delicious, Gloria, you are a very fine cook," said Ross.

"Thank you Ross, I appreciate your helpfulness."

After cleaning the kitchen, Ross left to go back home. He did not mention anything about trying to hold Gloria's hand. He would take it slow and easy. He did not want to push her away. He knew that it had to be God's timing. Gloria did seem to be healing.

John had been talking with a couple of people at church that knew of a poor family that needed help to repair the roof on their house. John asked Rae and Ryon if they could help mend the roof. John went over to find the family in need. He rode up to their house and found the man outside in his garden. "Hello," called out John. "I heard that your roof is caving in. My brothers and I would like to help. May I take a look at it and access the damage? It will cost you nothing. We do mission work around the neighborhood and it will be our pleasure."

"Well, I am not sure. I usually do not accept charity. I don't have the funds to have it repaired and my three children are young. I know that my wife would appreciate your help. I suppose so, I will appreciate it too. I need to learn to allow others to help me," said Eric. "It is that I have been independent most of my life, it is hard to depend on others. Maybe I just need to learn a lesson from this, thank you."

"By the way, my name is John Ingram. I represent County Church."

"I am Eric Chestnut. It is my pleasure to meet you. Come around to the back and I will show you the roof." They walked to the back of the house.

"I see. My brothers and I will be back in two days and get this all repaired for you."

John left and talked to Rae and Ryon. They were more than willing to help.

"I would want someone to help me in need. Claire and I are having another baby and I would accept all the help that I could get to keep my family safe."

"Congratulations," said Rae and John at the same time.

The men picked up the materials for the roof at the merchantile store the next day.

"D'Anna will you and the children come with us when we fix the roof on Eric's house? They have three children and two of them are about the ages of Matthew and Luke. You can get acquainted with Eric's wife to see if they have any special needs for the children."

"That is a wonderful idea. Matthew and Luke can take them a few play toys. I will talk with them about sharing their toys. I am sure that Ms Dillon will keep Angie for us."

That night before bed D'Anna got down on the floor to play with Matthew, who was now six and Luke was four. Time was slipping by.

"Matthew and Luke, I have a small suggestion for you two boys. Tomorrow morning your Uncle Rae, Uncle Ryon and your dad are going to help a family in need. The children do not have many toys and how would you two like to share yours with them?"

"Mom, I will pick out something that I belive that they will like. Hope they are boys,"said Matthew.

"There are two boys about your and Luke's age and the baby is a girl from what your dad says. That sounds like our family."

"Then I will give the older one my toy horse and buggy. I like playing with it and believe that he will too. What about you Luke, what will you give?" asked Matthew.

"I like playing with my toy horses and the caral with the barn. I will give them to the other boy." Luke wanted to out give his brother.

"Let us gather them together and I will wrap them up and you guys can present them to the children tomorrow. I am so proud of you two, Matthew and Luke. Did you know that you are following the golden rule?"

"I remember that from Sunday School," said Matthew. "It says something like, do unto others as you would have them do unto you. I would want them to share their toys with me."

Early the next morning the families gathered together with their wagons full of supplies and headed out toward Eric's. When they got there, Eric met them at the door and invited D'Anna and the boys in. He called out to his wife, Carol, and allowed the women to introduce themselves while he went out to start work on the roof with the men..

"Hello, my name is D'Anna and these are my sons, Matthew and Luke. My baby girl is with the baby sitter."

"I am Carol and these boys are my sons Eric Junior and Peter."

The boys saw each other and Matthew and Luke handed them their presents. The boys tore into their presents and they all sat on the floor to play ranch.

"That went over well," said Carol. "Please D'Anna come on in. I was just about to make tea while the baby is sleeping. Eric said that y'all would be coming over. It is a pleasure to meet you and your family."

"Eric runs a vegetable farm and we sell vegetables at the flea market. I make pies and can fruits to sell. We eat well with the garden. Eric is a very good farmer. He has a green thumb. We are still young at the business but hope to continue to grow in the future. We need to make it work so that we will be able to hire farm hands. We are off to a good start. We just need more time into the making. Eric will be planting potatoes and strawberries next year. We also are starting a few citrus fruit trees, but that will take time."

"Thatl sounds like a good plan. I will pray that it all works out. Let us know how we may help you. We would like to buy fruits and vegetables from you too. I will mention it to the church ladies and I am sure that they will buy also. We do need a farmers market here."

The time flew by and it was time to go home.

Before they left Carol said, "hold on jus a minute." She went into the house and came back with a box of canning jars. Inside were twelve pint jars of strawberry jelly. She handed them to D'Anna. "Please share these with your family and especially the wives of Rae and Ryon. We wish that we were able to pay you for the new roof. Please come when you can for vegetables. You and your families are welcome at any time."

"Good day," said Eric as Rae, John, and Ryon were preparing to leave. "I can not repay you for such a fine job you all did with the roof. I thank you from the bottom of my heart. I run a vegetable farm and sell the vegetables and hopefully later,fruit, at the farmers market. It is so far away that Carol and I were thinking about opening our own market. Please come anytime and get vegetables from us. I have a fifty pound bag of potatoes that I want to give you." Eric walked to the dirt mound in the back of the yard and brought back the bag of potatoes. "These potatoes are the best around. They have a delicious taste. They sell very well."

"Thank you," said Rae. "I am sure that our families will enjoy them. I will just have to come back for more and bring the neighbors. By the way, you live quite a ways from County Church. If you are in the neiighborhood, please drop by and join us. Our pastor is the best in the state and we enjoy his sermons. Our town is a better place because of him."

6

Saturday was booming at the merchantile store. Everyone was very busy. Alex Mansfield kept eying Gloria. He would pick up a tool and pretend to be studying it but looking at Gloria the whole time. Ross caught Alex in the motion. Ross began to feel a little jealous. Alex was much younger than he was and a very good looking man. He knew that Alex went on many business trips and wasn't always around. When Alex went to the cash register to check out, he started flirting with Gloria. She seemed to be a little embarrassed but she smiled and acted friendly. "What is such a pretty lady doing working in a hardware store. You should be a princess in a castle," said Alex. "I will come by to see you again."

Gloria just waved him on by and kept on working. Ross was thinking that Gloria could have any man that she wanted. He did not want to feel jealous. He knew that true love was in God's hands. Later on he would talk to Gloria about how he felt. It had been a year since he had met her and Bobby and he had waited long enough. He wanted to let her know before someone else took her away.

Ross did not know it but Gloria was feeling closer and closer to him. He was a very Godly man and showed compassion to the shoppers in his store. If someone needed something but could not afford it, Ross would lower the price. She noticed that he had even given away a few tools. He was very kind to Bobby. He loved him in as his own son. She had wondered why Ross was single. Maybe she would ask him one day.

7

Rae was thinking about retiring from the Bank. He was so busy at the ranch. It was cheaper to quit his job at the bank than hiring another accountant. He was able to do his own accounting but he just did not have the time with his bank job and running the ranch. He needed to talk to Lizzy first to find her interest in the matter. After supper, with the children in bed, Rae asked Lizzy to set on the sofa with him. He needed to communicate a matter with her.

"Elisa, my Lizzy, I have been thinking about retiring from the bank. There is just too much work around the ranch that is very important. I do not have the time to work both jobs. I feel that the ranch is more important to us. I believe that we will be saving money if I quit the bank job. I just can't see anyone else running my accounting system. Of course, D'Anna could do it. She was always brilliant in math but she is so busy with her own family. Besides, I think that I will wait for the twentieth year there and retire. There are a few incentitives."

"Rae, thank you for asking me. I trust you in all that you do. You are a wonderful provider for our family. It will be good to see you around here more often. I do miss you when you are away. You will even have more time with the children and you can teach Willy and Lilly how to run the ranch. You know that they are getting older."

"Yes, they are old enough now to get familiar with the accounting business and even running the ranch. They have finished school through the sixth grade and I would like to send them to a college that they prefer. I want them to continue on in their education. We will talk to them very soon about this. Willy will worry a little about Bark. I will assure Willy that I will take very good care of his dog. Bark has been a good protector. He warned Willy about a snake that was close by the other day when he was helping me with the chores. Bark went after the snake and scared it away. Bark has turned out to be a good investment after all."

When The Sewing Circle got together, they would always compare notes. "Abby, I got a letter from Lorisa. Lesley is taking a train to New York on a business trip and Lorisa is traveling with him. Their nanny is taking care of Billy and Paul. I pray that they will have safe travels," said D'Anna.

"I pray so too," said Abby. "It will be good for them to have a holiday together. Lorisa has worked so faithfully taking care of the boys, her home, teaching piano lessons and sewing for for her church charity. I hope she tells us all about it when she returns."

"I visited New York once with father and mother. By the way, my parents are coming for a visit in the near future. I surely will be glad to see them. I miss them and Theresa and Ryon Junior will be happy to see them. My parents always spoil them whenever they come for a visit. New York is lovely. I enjoyed the scenery on the way there," said Claire.

"I will have to ask Joe to let that be our next trip. I believe that Lorisa will enjoy her travels,"said Lydia.

"Lorisa enjoys adventure as well as the rest of us. Our children are slowing down our adventure trips. But we get plenty of adventures with our children and I enjoy that as much as traveling," said Lizzy. "Let's surprise Lorisa and make Billy and Paul some new clothes. The clothes will arrive at her home by carrier about the time she returns."

Lesley and Lorisa boarded the train for New York. "Lorisa, we will make many stops on the way to New York. Be prepared to feel free to look around the towns where we stop. We will have a few minutes before the train starts out again. This way you get to have a short visit in some of the shopping stores," said Lesley.

"That shounds fantastic. I will take everything in. You just make sure that you stay right by my side. I am getting excited. Remember the last train trip that we took. It was our honeymoon and the scenery was beautiful. Every little town had it's own different cultures. It was fun just to listen to so many different accents and dialets. And how about that show boat on the grand old Mississippi. What a trip to remember. I will never forget it."

"That was a great trip. One of my favorites. To me,it was all about you. I am pleased that we are here together. Just you and me once again. We have been so busy. I am glad that you came with me. We will buy souviners for the children and their nanny."

Lorisa and Lesley were enjoying their trip together. They had stopped at several towns on the way to New york. In Pennsylvania, the train stopped again to pick up passangers. But one passenger was a very special one. As the lovely woman boarded the train and walked down the aisle, she spotted a young lady that looked just like her mother. Marian kept staring at her. She had to hold on to a seat, afraid of fainting. After Marian found her set across from the young lady and her husband, she settled her bags in the upper compartment, she could only think. This young beautiful lady brought back many memories of her childhood on her family's plantation. Marian could not help it. She just had to inquire of this young woman. After the train was well on it's way, Marian turned to the young gentleman and asked him. "Sir,if I may, can I ask you to change seats with me for a moment. I would love to talk to your beautiful wife."

Lesley tod her, "just a moment and I will ask Lorisa if that is okay with her." Lesley turned toward Lorisa, "Lorisa, the lady next to me would like to change seats with me for a few moments so that she could talk with you. Is that alright with you?"

Lorisa peered around Lesley and spied Marian. "Yes, Lesley, that will be fine but don't stay away too long."

So Lesley changed seats with Marian. Marian introduced herself to Lorisa. "Dear lady, my name is Marian Jefferson Smith. Not to alarm you but you look just like my long deceased mother, Eleanor Jefferson."

"My name is Lorisa Jefferson Vanderbilt. It is a pleasure to meet you. We do have the same maiden name. Where are you from? Do you know any Jefferson's? My father never mentioned that we had kin in the states. My family was born in Mexico but my father was born in Georgia."

"Georgia, yes, so was I. Is your father's name William Jefferson? William is my brother and we got separated during the Civil War. That was many years ago."

"Why, yes, that was my father's name. Are we talking about the same William Jefferson. He never told us to much about his life or his childhood. We knew that he was a southern gentleman and he taught all of us children how to survive and make a home for ourselves."

"I am positive that we are talking about the same William. You are the split image of our mother. The same dark auburn hair, the same peridot eyes, and the creamy complextion. I wish that you could have met her. Mother and father passed away during the Civil War. Those were very hard years for us. My beau took me away to Pennsylvania to save me. We got married and I never heard from William again. We did not know how to find him. Now you tell me that he traveled to Mexico after the war. I wonder what took him there? Please tell me about my brother and all of his family. I am anxious to know. I really have missed him. He was my big brother and protector. He would not allow a guy to get near me. But when he left to go to war, I met Daniel. We fell in love. Daniel was kinda like William, a big protector. He did save me and I always have been thankful every since. He passed away several months ago and I miss him tremendously. I am going to New York to visit my only relatives, my mother-in-law, Regina, and my daughter, JoLynn, and my grandaugher, Annette. Regina is getting very old and feeble, I wanted to see her one last time. You are my very own niece. Tell me more."

"My father and mother had six children. We are all living except for Billy. He died when he was only ten years old. He was the joy of our lives. We were all so devastated. We have never completely gotton over the accident. We have a special memorial for him every Christmas when the family gets together for a Christmas family reunion. We all still miss him. All of the children have families of their very own and we just keep growing and multiplying. You have a very large family to get to know, Aunt Marian. This will be a surprise to everyone. Oh, what a marvelous surprise. I can hardly wait for them all to meet you. Please give me your address so that we can keep in contact. Christmas is not far away. Would you possibly be able to come to our next Christmas family reunion? It will be wonderful. I may just keep this a secret until that special day. If I can. It will be very hard. Since I live a couple of days from the rest of my brothers and sisters, I believe that I can manage."

"I will be there. Nothing can hold me back. Please tell me about all of them. If your handsome husband will allow us to talk for a while."

Lorisa peered over Marian to talk to Lesley. She introduced Marian to Lesley. "What a delightful surprise," said Lesley. "No wonder you wanted to talk to Lorisa."

"Lesley, dear, may I impose on you for a few more monents? We have a lot of catching up to do. Lorisa and I are excited to know that we are kin. I just found out that I am her aunt. New York is not far now and I will return her at a proper time. This is so important to me."

"Of course, I would feel the same. Please have a historial conversation. I will be fine. I hope to see you more often in the future."

"Oh, thank you Lesley. May I call you Lesley. You are already family."

"Please do and I will call you Aunt Marian. How does that sound."

"That, my dear, is music to my ears."

Turning back to Lorisa, "Now Lorisa, we have a lot to talk about. Let us start with William. Please tell me all about my brother."

"Aunt Marian, it sounds so good to call you my aunt. Your brother met my mother, Angelina in Mexico after the war. He built a house for us and they had six children together. My father traveled back and forth from Mexico to the states because of his job all of those years. He taught us how to be good stewards of all of our posessions. He was a wonderful provider. When he was home with us he taught all of his children to be survivors. The girls learned how to ride a horse, sew and knit, and how to manage good business. He taught the boys how to ride, to shoot, how to manage money, and how to be proper southern gentlemen. He taught us very well. My mother and grandmother taught us all how to run their cafe. We were taught how ro raise chickens for their eggs and meat. We sold chickens, eggs, and chicken feathers to buy stock for the cafe. It helped us when we moved to the states to start a ranch of our very own. After we were young adults, we never saw father again for a very long time. Then all of a sudden he showed up at our ranch. His health was failing him. He had given our mother a wooden cross necklace and we named the ranch after his and my mother's gift; The Circle Cross Ranch. She cherished that wooden cross. When my father died, he was found clutching the cross to his chest. I will have to tell you the story when we get together again. Rae is the oldest. We left Mexico when he turned eighteen. We felt that we did not belong in the neighborhood anymore because we are a mixed race. Our friends started treating us a little differently than when we were children. We were different. Father had taught us a little different than our friends culture because he grew up as a southern gentleman. D'Anna is the oldest girl. Then there is Abby, Ryon, me, and there was Bily. We are all married and we all have children of our own. That makes you a great aunt. Everyone will be so glad to meet you. I can hardly wait."

Aunt Marian and Lorisa exchanged adresses. "Here we are at the New York depot. Lorisa I will keep in touch and hopefully see you and your---my family at Christmas. Maybe you should tell them about me. I do not want it to be a shock to them. Praise God for letting us meet. I know that He has great things in store for all of us. I will tell JoLynn that she has cousins that we had never heard of before. She has a daughter, Annette, that is about twenty years old now. I will be in touch soon. Lesley, thank you for letting me borrow my niece for a time. I pray that you both have a safe trip."

"Thank you Aunt Marian. I look forward to seeing you again."

"I will visit at Christmas, we are all family. I am so happy that God led us together."

Lorisa and Aunt Marian hugged goodby. They left the depot going in different directions.

"Lesley, I can hardly wait to get back home to tell my siblings about this wonderful news. They will be as surprised as I am. If only father were here to see her too."

"Lorisa, I want to take you to a Broadway play while we are in the city. We will visit Carnegie Hall and walk down Central park. There are many sites to behold but we can not see them all in three days. If you would like and enjoy New York we can make another trip at another time."

"Lesley, I will take in everything that I can and get brochures on the events and places."

Gloria and Bobby had been working for Ross in his merchantile store for over a year. Gloria began to see Ross for the man that he was. So generous and patient. He also had a very manly physic and she noticed how good looking he was. She found herself every morning ready to go to work to be around Ross. She was especially glad of how Bobby had taken to Ross. Ross treated Bobby like his very own son. When Bobby needed to talk to someone he would go to Ross instead of her. "Bobby, you know that you can still come to your mother when you have questions. I am here for you whenever you need to talk."

"Mom, I am getting older now and some questions are just for us men. Ross is like the father that I never had. He is good to me. He has taught me many things and I enjoy being around him. Why don't you and Ross get married and we all can be a family."

"Bobby! Where in the world did you get that from? You know that we are his employees. He may not appreciate such a suggestion."

"Oh, mom, you know that Ross likes you. He has commented on how pretty you are and how much he admires you. I see you eying him at times here lately. Why not? He is a good spiritual man and I would not mind being his son."

"Bobby, I will dismiss everything that I have heard you say. Go along now and finish your work." But Gloria was thinking that Bobby was not far from the truth. She did like Ross too.

That day in the store, business went on as usual until Alex Mansfield walked in. Ross saw him come in. Ross walked over to him to see if he needed any help. "Hello Alex, how may I help you today."

"Actually, I came in to see Gloria. Oh, there she is." Alex walked over to find Gloria straightening the material on the table. Ross held his breath as Alex walked over to see Gloria. It was her choice and he would not stop her from her happiness if that was the case. He wanted her to be happy. "Hi, Gloria, how are you doing this fine day?"

"Hello Mr. Mansfield. It is a fine day and I am enjoying it very much."

"Gloria, please call me Alex. We have known each other for a time now. I came to ask you if you would like to have supper with me this evening? You can choose the time and I will be here to escort you to Katie's."

"Thank you Alex. I do appreciate the invite but I have already made plans for this evening."

"I am sorry to hear that. I will come back at a more convenient time. Good day, I will see you later." At that Alex walked out of the store.

Ross pretended to be busy but he heard every word. He was so relieved. He had to say something to Gloria. "Gloria, you know that you are free to see whomever you wish. I have been a little slow about asking you out myself. I would love for us and Bobby to have supper out one evening. Would you object to have an evening out together?"

"Ross, how about this evening?"

Ross did not want her to know that he had just heard her turn Alex down for the evening. He was a little surprised.

"That sounds like a winner. After work we can walk down to Katie's and have a nice meal. I believe that she has roast beef on Thursday's."

"Then it is a date. I will inform Bobby."

"Inform me about what?" Bobby had just walked around the corner from the back room where he was taking inventory.

"Your mother, you, and I will walk down to Katie's and have supper together. How does that sound? She serves roast beef on Thursday's."

"It is about time we all got together," said Bobby. Then he walked away smiling.

That evening Gloria, Bobby, and Ross enjoyed their roast beef meal with creamed potatoes and creamed corn with Katie's delicious biscuits. Biscuits that could not be resisted. They all had casual talk and the supper was over much too soon.

When Ross walked beside of Gloria to go home, he took her hand in his. She in turn held his hand. Bobby noticed and his smile was even larger. When they walked to the door to go home, Bobby ran ahead of them to give them a chance to be alone."Thank you for the delicious meal, Ross. I enjoyed us all being together." He then ran up the stairs to his home.

Ross and Gloria lingered a little at the door. "I really enjoyed this evening, Gloria. I hope that we can have many more evenings together." He then kissed her on the forward and turned to his own door.

Gloria felt the tingle in her heart and walked slowly up the stairs.

That night Bobby woke up Gloria. "Mom do you hear that noise. It sounds like it is coming from down stairs."

"Now that you mention it, Bobby, I do hear it. Listen, be quiet, it is coming from the back right corner of the store."

"Knock on the wall and see if Ross heard anything. He may be sleeping but I believe that his bedroom wall is next to our living room," said Bobby.

Gloria knocked on the wall. "Ross, we hear a noise downstairs. Ross, Ross."

Ross stepped to the wall and asked, "What is it."

"We hear a noise down stairs, can you come over and investigate? Only you have a gun. Bobby and I are afraid to go down stairs."

"I will be right over," said Ross. Ross dressed himself, found his pistol and walked down his stairs to the building next door. He had built an inside door from one store to the other for easy access to his inventory. When Ross got down stairs he turned on the electric lights that he had installed, being happy for electricity. When Bobby heard Ross downstairs he opened his door and walked down the stairs himself with Gloria behind him.

Bobby saw something jump and called out. "Hey Ross, over here. It is just a cat. It must have come in when we had the door open. It is just trying to find a way out."

Ross opened the back door to the store and shooded the cat outside.

"Ross we were sorry to wake you, but we did not know what it was," said Gloria.

"No problem, I am glad that you did. It could have been anything. I am relieved that it was not a bugler. I am not sure how I would have dealt with that."

Actually Ross was just happy to see Gloria again that evening. "I'll tell you what. Anytime that you need me just knock on the wall as you did a while ago. We can use that as our secret communication."

"That sounds like a mystery. Be prepared for more communication," said Gloria.

"Anytime," said Ross. "Now you two run back up stairs and get some more sleep. I will check out everything here and lock the back door. Remember to call on me when you feel like it. Good night Bobby, good night Gloria."

Bobby and Gloria walked back home up the stairs happy that all was well.

The next day Gloria and Ross teased each other about a cat scaring them all. They were enjoying each other's company. Gloria, Bobby, and Ross had many evenings out after that.

Bobby was talking with Ross down at the fishing stream. "Ross why don't you and mom get married. You two seem to get along very well."

"Bobby,I have thought about it many times. I wanted to be sure that your mother was ready for another husband. I am still not sure. But I will never find out if I don't ask her, hugh?"

"Ask and see what she says. Just talk with her and don't hide anything from her. My mom is a truth person. But just between you and me. I know that she is very fond of you. She has mentioned what a great husband and dad that you would make. She even once mention why you were a sinle man."

"I would love for you to be my son, Bobby. I have grown to love you and your mother. I will talk with her about my past. Y'all will not have to wonder about anything."

"Okay, when we have supper together this evening, I will excuse myself and go home early. That will give y'all some time to talk,"said Bobby.

That evening when the meal was almost over, Bobby excused himself telling his mother that he wanted to finish a project that he was working on before the next day. He was building a sail boat in a bottle and wanted to put it on display for sale the next morning. He had been working on It for three days and he knew a couple of boys that wanted to buy it.

After the meal, Ross walked Gloria back home. Before she went upstairs he wanted to talk to her. "Gloria, will you come to the kitchen in the back of the store and have coffee with me. I would like to tell you a little about my past life?"

"Yes, Ross, I have been curious about why you are still a single man."

Ross made coffee for Gloria and himself and handed her a cup. "You still make a good cup of coffee," commented Gloria.

"Thank you Gloria. I have been making coffee for twenty years now. I am an old pro. One reason that I wanted to talk with you is to let you know about my past. My father started this store when I was just a baby. My parents worked very hard to make a go of it. I have remolded the store several times to keep up with progress. It started off as a trading post. It has come a long way. I went to school here in this town. There were thirty children in my class. The class had all ages, from six to sixteen years of age. Even the older children wanted to learn to read and write. I fell in love with one of my classmates. She was a lovely girl. Her parents were poor with many children. She missed school many days because she always seemed to be sick. The doctor did not know what was wrong with her. She always had many colds. But I liked her anyway. We got married and moved in with my parents. All was well at the beginning, then Linda got sick again. The doctor kept her in bed for a while. She had consumption terribly. After we were married three months, Linda died. I was heartbroken. It took a long time to get over. I was not interested in any other women. Time just kept passing by and here I am still a single man. I guess, I stayed too busy with the store to make a go of it that I never pursued another wife until now. Gloria, I have fallen in love with you. I know that I am a little older than you. It would be my pleasure for you to be my wife. I love Bobby as a son already. We get along so very well. I would like for him to inherit this store if he so chooses. What I am saying, Gloria, will you marry me and become my wife?"

"Ross, I have never met a man like you. You are the kind of man that I would love to have as a husband. I have been a little afraid of a second marriage. My first husband was kind when we first met, then he changed. I have been reluctant. Yes, I would love to be your wife."

Ross was so happy. "Stay right here." Ross went into the store behind the front desk, pulled out a box that he had placed in the bottom drawer and returned to find Gloria refreshing their coffee. "Gloria, I want to make this right." He opened the box, took out the beautiful engagement ring and placed it on Gloria's ring finger.

"Ross, the ring is beautiful. Let's go tell Bobby."

Ross and Gloria walked up the stairs to Gloria's apartment to call for Bobby. Bobby had heard them walk up the stairs and met them at the door. Bobby reached for Gloria's left hand and saw the beautiful engagement ring. "It is about time this happened. I have been praying about it for several months. This prayer has been answered. I am happy for you both and for me too."

That night when Gloria was in her apartment, she knocked on the wall. "Ross can you hear me?" Ross heard the knock and Gloria's voice. It seemed a little strange to be talking through the wall.

"Yes, I hear you. Are you okay over there."

"Yes we are okay, I just wanted to say that I love you through the wall."

"I love you too and it does feel a little strange to be talking through a wall but I like it," said Ross.

The next day, Lizzy and D'Anna came into the store to set up the dress display. Gloria was all ready for them. Everything was in place. Gloria had decorated the walls with lovely colors and pctures. She already had a window display half finished.

"Hi Gloria, you are making the dress room very lovely. Are the pictures for sale too? They are very exquisite. Do we have an artist in town?"

"Yes we do. Mr. Randy Blake paints land-scape paintings. He paints from all different directions. I love the pictures of the creek, stream, lake, and the animal sceens."

"I thought that they looked familiar. I recognize all of these places. He is doing a fantastic job. I will have to buy one for our foyer. Maybe I can get him to paint our very own yard. D'Anna, Lydia, Claire, and Abby will be meeting us here in a few minutes. Is that a diamond that I see on your hand? Hold is up and let me see. It is beautiful, congratulations. I bet that I can guess who gave it to you. I am so happy for you."

Gloria held up her hand for Lizzy to see. "I am happy too. Ross is a good man and I can see God opening the doors for our marriage." Lizzy hugged Gloria.

Here come the girls now. The sisters walked into the dress room and inspected all that was in the room. "This room looks fantastic. It will attrack many eyes," said D'Anna.

"You have missed one extremely important inspection," said Lizzy to them. The sisters looked at her as to say-what are you talking about. Gloria held up her left hand and all the sisters walked over to look at Gloria's engagement ring. They all marveled over the ring and told her congratulations.

"We have something to talk with you about, Gloria. When D'Anna got married, she, me, and Lorisa made her a beautiful wedding gown. Lizzy and Claire have their own. The dress has been worn by D'Anna, me, Lorisa, and Lydia. What if you come over to Lizzy's sewing room and allow us to remake the dress to your liking," said Abby. "As D'Anna says, this dress has been made with many prayers and whoever wears it wil live a happy life. We all can vouch for that."

All of The Sewing Circle agreed and coaxed her to come. "I just got engaged last night. That does sound good. Thank you all for the suggestion. I will come over and see what we all can do. I will be very proud to wear a wedding gown made by the most brilliant seamstresses in the state, The Sewing Circle."

"Have you set the wedding date?" asked Lydia. "I also have worn my wedding dress made from those same materials. I felt like a queen."

"Ross said anytime was all right with him."

"Then we will not waste time. You go ahead and set the date. We will help you with everything, The invitations, the reception, and the wedding," said Claire.

Ross helped everyone set up the racks for display. The sisters had brought over dresses and shirts that they had made and hung them on the racks. Gloria finished the display with the maniquins and all was set. They all stood back to look at the new dress room. Gloria had made a small sign to place in the display window that read. Designs by The Sewing Circle. "Thank you for the sign," said D'Anna. "We did not expect you to do that."

"It is my pleasure. Everyone should know who the designers are. You are all so good at what you do. I am proud to display your dress designs," said Gloria.

The Sewing Circle stayed busy making clothes for the dress shop. Everyone got a commission on the clothes that were sold. Fashions were becoming more modern and the dress shop was a booming business. It was another asset to the merchantile shop. The dress shop became so expansive that it became a store within itself. Gloria stayed busier than ever.

Ross was talking to Gloria one evening. "Gloria you stay so busy. When we get married, I do not want you here all day long. I want you to have some free time to do as you please. Let us hire another lady to help run the dress shop to free you up a little."

"It is getting a little overwhelming. Some help will be great. We can afford to hire someone since the shop is doing a good business. We are planning to display a ferfume and fragrance bar soon."

"That is a good idea. Where did you get that idea?"

"D'Anna and Lizzy said that Aunt Jame taught them how to make their own soaps with different fragrances. Aunt Jame has made many a bar. She has wrapped them with fancy paper and she will bring them over in a couple of days. I have a feeling that it will go over big. We also will sell stylish ladies shoes. Teresa and her family are making mocassions and leather vests. I believe that it wll be a big hit."

"You are still a wonder, Gloria. You and your ideas have increased the inventory and assets to a high margin level. So what date are we getting married?"

"The date is set two months from today. Is that okay with you?"

"Today would be soon enough," said Ross.

"Everything is all set. The wedding dress is almost finished. The Sewing Circle has been working overtime to get it just right. I do not know what I would have done without The Sewing Circle. They have worked harder than I have. It is good to have such wonderful friends. Have you asked Pastor Joe Hodges if he would preform the honors?"

"He said that he would be happy to; just let him know the date. I will go tell him now."

Later that day, Alex walked into the store. He thought that he would try one more time to ask Gloria out. Ross noticed Alex walk in. He grabbed a few can goods from the stock room to add them to the shelves. Alex walked over to Gloria. She was working with some papers by the cash register. She made sure that Alex could see her hands as she was working.

"Hi Gloria, I am in town for a few days and"-----as he was talking he noticed the engagement ring on Gloria's hand. "You are engaged? Well, hats off to the lucky man."

Gloria looked at Alex, smiled and said, "I am the blessed one Alex." At that Alex turned around and walked out of the store.

Ross just walked back out to the stock room and gathered more canned goods.

10

Lorisa and Lesley returned home a few weeks later. They had bought toys and clothes for the children and a shawl for the nanny. Lesley and Lorisa loved up on Billy and Paul then played with them for a while. Billy was so happy to see his parents. "Mother, father, you can not leave us again. The next time Paul and I are going with you. We did have fun with Miss Gilbert though."

"The next time, Billy, we will all go together. We missed you two so much," said Lorisa.

"Lorisa, I know that you are just dying to wirte your sisters and brothers letters about your Aunt Marian. Tomorrow you have the day off so that you can get all those letters addressed. It is a good thing that you canceled your piano lessons for another week."

"Thank you dear. You are right. I will start first thing in the morning. Right now I am ready for some rest and relaxation. Let's get the children into bed."

The next morning, Lorisa wasted no time to start her letter writing. She would write each sibling. She loved to tell the story over and over again.

Since the siblings lived close by, they all got their letters a week later on the same day. Lorisa had written them all about the same thing.

Dear brother Rae,

"I pray that this letter finds you well. You will not believe this but you have an aunt. Her name is Marian Jefferson Smith. William (father) and Marian were separated during the Civil War. When the war got close to the Jefferson plantation, Marian's beau took her to New York to keep her safe. He is a hero in my eyes. He died a few months ago.

Anyway, I met Marian on the train when we stopped to pick up passangers in Pennsylvania. She recognized me because she said that I am the splitting image of our grandmother, Eleanor Jefferson. She pleaded for me to tell her all about her brother. I told her what I knew. She is coming to our Christmas family reunion this year and each of you can tell her more about father. I was younger and did not get to know much about him. I could not keep it a secret untill Christmas. She asked about all of y'all. She will get the full story of father when she visits.

In the meantime we will get to hear more about our father. I can hardly wait to see her again. We all have a lot of catching up to do. Her late husband's mother, Regina, and Marian's daughter, JoLynn live in New York. JoLynn has a daughter named Annette. I hope to get to meet them also. I will write JoLynn a letter and invite her to our Christmas family reunion. Isn't it great that God allowed us to find our long lost aunt and cousins that we knew nothing about? I will close with this because I am writing all of you individually. If not before, I will see you all at Christmas."

Love and prayers, Lorisa

P S " Tell Lizzy thank you very much for the clothes. They were at the post office when we arrived back home. They all are very lovely. We all will enjoy wearing them."

After everyone read their letters, they could not wait to get together to discuss their long lost aunt. What could they do though. What could they say. It did not matter. It was a good time to get together. Rae and Lizzy invited all of the family to their house the next day for supper. Aunt Jame and Uncle Eli were tickled to have all of the family over. They cooked a special ham and turkey supper even though it was not Thanksgiving or Christmas. It was a special ocassion. They wished that Lorisa could be there.

Rae said at the supper table, "It is good for us all to be together. How many tables do we need now? Wow, we are really growing. Whoever wishes, is welcome to spend the night. I want to thank Aunt Jame and Uncle Eli for the wonderful meal on such a short notice. They have never failed us and we all love them dearly. Lorisa did not say a lot in her letter other than she has found father's sister. I can hardly wait to meet her. We have a lot to tell her but she has a lot to tell us too. I guess she will be a few years younger than father. JoLynn will be about our age or a little older and Annette, I am not sure yet. I will write her and tell her to bring her family with her and they can stay as long as they would like."

"It may take a while since we all have so many stories," said Abby. "Just think, our very own aunt. I am getting excited to see her. I will write her and let her know how much she is welcomed here. Juan said that he may come visit with us in the spring of next year. He is so busy at the cafe. His hired help is very good at managing the cafe and Juan said that he would trust him completely to run the cafe for a few months. It will be good to see mother's brother too. We have not seen our uncle in ages."

"Now you are making me very excited, Abby. I am anxious to see Aunt Marian, her family and Uncle Juan and his family. We have a lot of preparing to do. I would like to present them with gifts to take back home. I will write JoLynn also to get her and Annette's measurements for the clothes that The Sewing Circle will make," said D'Anna.

"I will make sure that they have a good visit at my farm," said Ryon. "We will have a barbecue when they come, after Christmas of course."

"I will be glad to do anything that I can to help," said Lizzy. "The sewing room is always open to anyone that wants to come any day."

"I will pick out some nice fabric for them all. Gloria has such an assortment of many varieties now," said Claire.

"We should get together more often. Maybe we can find a good time in the summer. We can go down to the lake with a huge picnic, swim, and fish for our supper. The bridge is built sturdy and we have a couple of picnic tables there. I am building a bath house with a kitchen and a large dining room with a bar. Similiar to the one in the house. The lake has a special place made for swimming. Of course, you can go there any time. It belongs to all of us. I am also expanding the lake. The natural spring makes it good for drinking water. Our ranch hands finished building the pump yesterday. The lake stays cool during the hot weather. John and Ryon are pitching in to make it a home vacation." Rae was still looking out for his family and seeing into the future.

It was getting late so everyone went back to their homes with a new joy in their hearts.

11

Sunday was a decison making day. Bobby asked Pastor Hodges about being baptised. Pastor Hodges explained to Bobby about the death, burial, and ressurection of Jesus. "Now that you have accepted Jesus Christ as your personal Savior, Bobby, the next step will be baptism by water submersion. This represents that you will submit your beliefs to the public and live a Christian life for all to see. We all have to prove ourselves. We do that by the actions that we take and the choices that we make. We imitate Jesus by trusting and obeying Him."

"I am ready to do that Pastor. I want to be baptised before my mom and Ross get married. I want to prove that Jesus lives in my heart as the Holy Spirit. God will always be with me and I want to be the son that will be pleasing to our Father."

"Willy and Lilly will also be baptised at the same time. You will not be alone, although I know that you know that anyway. I will baptist you and the others in the creek behind the church. There is a deep spot there where the town children have made a pool for themselves. It is the perfect spot. I have had many baptisms there before. Wear what you would like and bring a change of clothes. Next Sunday after church we will meet there. We can all follow one another. There will be much singing. The ladies are making picnic dinners for everyone."

That Sunday had arrived and Bobby was excited. He wanted the whole world to know that he loved the Lord. He talked to Willy for a few minutes. "Willy, I am glad that we are getting baptised together. I am happy that we are friends and we will always share this memory together. Is Lilly excited to be baptised too?"

"Pastor Hodges said that Luke will help us with everything and he will tell us what to do. He has helped his dad many times and I am glad for his help. We will not be in the dark. Lilly is as excited as I am. Nancy will be helping Lilly. She said that she was going to frame her baptismal clothes. Girls, what do you know about them anyway."

The baptismal went over very well. There were lots of food and lots of singing. It turned out to be a very rememberal day. Ross went up to Bobby and said, "Bobby, I am so proud of you. What a marvelous thing to commit to our Lord. Maybe we can help each other. I am here for you son." Gloria hugged her son, Bobby, and he went off to play with the other children around his age.

"Okay," said Eliza to Willy and Lilly. "In this family we are all accountable to one another. Let us keep the faith and continue on toward Heaven. Enduring till the end."

"That is a good way to put it," said Rae. We will all work together and be stronger through it all. I am very pleased with my family. Thank you Lizzy for all that you do, you are an inspiration to me."

"I love you Rae and we all inspire each other. I enjoy being with all of the family. This baptismal seems like a regular family reunion. Isn't it great?"

12

It was the middle of November. Ross and Gloria were ready for their wedding. County Church was packed. Pastor Hodges added a few extra words about the new family and about Bobby's testimony. The Sewing Circle had given Gloria and Ross a reception in the town hall. The Sewing Circle were standing together."D'Anna, Abby, Lydia, Lizzy, Claire, I can never repay you for all of all of the things that you have done for me. The reception room is so beautiful. Aunt Jame and Uncle Eli have out done themselves with the delicious food. They should own their own bakery. Also I thanked Janice and Ms Dillon for their input." Gloria hugged each member of The Sewing Circle. "I will never get over this. Thank you all so very much from the bottom of my heart for making this a success."

"We are glad that you like it all. We all enjoy giving parties and entertaining. Guess it is in our southern blood," said D'Anna. "You and Ross just enjoy this precious time together. Do not worry about anything whatsoever. We will take care of everything."

"Yes, please have a good time, we will take good care of Bobby. You know that he will be safe with us. Willy and Lilly can help him in the store and we will be their backups. The children can learn a lot from helping Bobby. I am glad that Bobby agreed to all of this. We will enjoy his company," said Lizzy.

"He will be treated like royalty. Aunt Jame and Uncle Eli will cook his favorite meals. Don't be surprised if he gains a little weight before y'all get back. I have to work extra hard to keep off their delicious food," commented Abby.

"We all will make sure that Bobby's ride back and forth to the store will be punctual. Bobby, Willy, and Lilly are able to hitch up the horse and buggy on their own. Now have fun and remember that Bobby will be fine," put in Claire.

"Especially enjoy the ride and the scenery and tell us all about it when y'all get back. We will be looking forward and praying for your safe return," said Lydia.

"I trust you all in everything. I will not worry at all. Thank you all again."

Gloria and Ross honeymooned in Houston. Bobby was old enough now that he could run the merchantile store by himself. The Jefferson's pitched in to help Bobby the week that his parents were gone. When the honeymooners got home, Ross remodled the upstairs to make one big large apartment for all of them. He tore out the wall between the two apartments and made extra space for his family. It was very lovely. Gloria redecorated their home making it look very modern to the times. Bobby was fourteen years old now. He was very efficient in the merchantile business. Ross was proud of his sufficientcy and trusted him with everything. They worked deligently together. Ross was happy to have a partner. Gloria continued to work as she liked but was flexible at any time.

D'Anna was the first to write Aunt Marian.

Dear Aunt Marian:

It is with great pleasure that I write this letter to you. When Lorisa wrote to tell us that we had an aunt, I was stunned but all so happy. We all miss mother and father very much and we all are looking forward to seeing you. Please bring JoLynn and her family when you come. Rae has a very large house. He built family rooms for each of us siblings and it is gorgeous. There is plenty of room. All of our family lives close together, next to Rae, except for Lorisa. She is not that far away, thank goodness.

We all are anxious to hear your stories about our father and his growing up years in your family. I will write JoLynn a personal invitation to join us at Christmas as I am you. Now that Christmas is only a month away, Rae and Ryon have already selected our Christmas tree. They so enjoy choosing and cutting down a special tree each year. Lorisa was unable to come home for Thanksgiving. We are looking forward to seeing her at Christmas. Write us and let us know about your situation and about JoLynn's. If we can assist you in any way feel free to let us know.

We are looking forward to your arrival. Let us know if we need to pick you up at the train depot. Remember that the weather here is not very cold in the winter months. You may want to pack you apparel lightly.

Until then, you are in my prayers. My prayers are also for safety travels. May God bless you and keep you safe.

Very truly yours,

D'Anna Ingram and family

Dean Cousin JoLynn,

I was very excited to hear that we (the Jefferson family) have a first and second cousin. I am sure that your mother has told you about us by now. We would love for you and your family to join us for our Jefferson Christmas family reunion on Christmas day. You may come as early as you would like. My brother Rae has a very large home and there is plenty of room for you to stay. You are welcome to stay as long as you wish. It will be so thrilling for all of us to be together. I am excited about meeting you and your family. I hope that you will be able to travel with your mother. We are looking forward for your stay. We have so much to share with you.

If we can help you in any way, please feel free to let us know. All of my brothers and sisters will be writing you. We do hope that you all can come. Write me and let me know about Annette and how old she is. I will be looking forward to your letter. Until then, may God bless you and your family. You all in in our prayers.

Very truly yours,

Cousin D'Anna

A few weeks later D'Anna received a letter from JoLynn.

> Dear Cousin D'Anna,
>
> It was a great pleasure receiving your letter and hearing from you. Mother, Annette, and I will be traveling a week before Christmas to Rae's ranch. He wrote mother and me to invite us to stay at his home when we arrive. He will meet us at the train depot and take us to his house. We all look forward to meeting you all also.
>
> Mother and I were very excited to learn about the Jefferson family. Mother has not gotten over it yet. It may take her a long time. She always talked about her brother William and wondered where he was. I am sorry to hear that he is deceased. I would so much liked to have met him. I look forward to seeing him in heaven. Thank you for inviting me to the Jefferson home. I look forward to meeting all of you in the near future. I may have to take notes, there are so many of you. But that is a very good thing. I always wanted brothers and sisters of my own. Now I can count you all as my family. My grandmother, on my father's side died a few weeks ago. Regina was eighty five years old. I will miss her greatly. Annette and I were living with her to help her out. My late husband died a year ago working with the railroad. Grandmother Regina willed her house to Annette and me. Mother will send a telegram to Rae as to the time of our arrival. Until then, you all are in my prayers also.
>
> Love and prayers,
>
> Cousin JoLynn and Annette

It was December and Christmas was coming. The Sewing Circle was busy making clothes. Christmas presents were wrapped and placed under the Christmas tree. The whole front wall was lined with presents.

The men in the family were busy cleaning up their homes to get ready for the big ocassion. They were all excited about this coming Christmas family reunion. It will be a very special time for all of them to remember and to write about. Lorisa and Lesley had arrived a few days early to visit each individual family seperately. They helped each family to prepare for the reunion. Lorisa wanted to feel the closeness to each of her brothers and sisters.

Rae and Lizzy drove their carriage to pick up Aunt Marian, cousin JoLynn, and second cousin Annette at the train depot.

"There they are, it has to be them. They look just like their description," said Lizzy. Rae and Lizzy walked up to Aunt Marian, JoLynn, and Annette and introduced themselves. "Aunt Marian, JoLynn, and Annette how wonderful to see you all." Lizzy and Rae hugged each one. "What a pleasure it is to have you come visit us. We all are so excited." Rae grabbed a couple of traveling cases and placed them in the carriage. Before he helped the ladies into the carriage he just looked at them and said, "My very own aunt. I am glad that you are here. Cousin JoLynn and Annette, how lovely you two are. Thank you for coming."

When Lorisa saw Rae pull the carriage up to the front door, she ran out to meet her aunt and cousins. "Aunt Marian, it is so good to see you again. Cousin JoLynn and Annette what a pleaseure to meet you. Come with me and I will show you all to your rooms." The group followed Lorisa inside the house and Lorisa led them upsairs to their rooms. "Would Annette like to have a room of her very own?"

"Thank you Lorisa, but Annette and I would like to room together if that is convenient," said JoLynn. "We love to talk together. Then if she gets bored she can choose another room at at later time."

"Of course it is; we have it set up either way. We are a large family and we always had guests spend the night when we were younger. That is before we all married and had families of our own," said Lorisa.

"Since it is getting late, I am sure that our travelers would like to freshen up. We will have a light refreshment and then we can all retire. We will catch up tomorrow after we have had our rest," Rae said.

Rae and Lizzy brought over finger sandwiches and tea with tea cakes from the kitchen that Aunt Jame had prepared.

"Tomorrow, Aunt Marian, one of the first things that I want to hear about is your hero. It is so romantic and I just have to hear all about it," said Lorisa. Every one said good night and the stories waited until the next day.

14

The next morning, everyone got reaquainted at the breakfast table. It was a few days before Christmas. Most all of the presents had been wrapped. Aunt Marian and JoLynn had added their presents to the ones already aligned around the Christmas tree and wall. "Rae, I do believe that you have hired the best cooks in the country. This is the best tasting breakfast that I have ever eaten and I have eaten many breakfasts. Your home is just gorgeous and JoLynn and I might just impose on you for a while longer. It is going to take time for us all to tell our stories. I want to hear every word," said Aunt Marian.

"Aunt Marian, JoLynn, and Annette, y'all are welcome to stay as long as you like and come visit at anytime. Our home is yours. I am sure that Lizzy will agree with me."

"I do agree with you Rae. It is a delight to have family visitors. We really should get together more often. Please, Aunt Marian, stay with us for a while."

After breakfast Rae and Lesley went out to work on some chores at the ranch. The Sewing Cirlce promised to meet later that morning to work on their sewing. When the sisters came, all the women gathered into the sewing room. The bigger children went outside to help work with ranch chores and the smaller children went to the play room with their babysitters and nannies. Lizzy showed Aunt Marian, JoLynn, and Annette around the sewing room and her sewing machine. As soon as the ladies got settled, one of the first things that Lorisa said was, "Now, Aunt Marian, I can wait no longer to hear about this hero. You have to tell us the story."

"I can tell the short version or the long version. I'm not sure if we have time for me to tell the long version. It took us weeks to get to our destination. It all started out after William signed up to be a soldier. Since he was a charta member of West Point, he joined the army as an officer. My family was very proud of him. He looked so handsome in his uniform with medals. My hero, as you call him met William at West Point. They became friends and Daniel came home with William for a visit. As soon as I met him, something just clicked inside of me. He was very dashing. His mannerism was lovingly charming. He was still at our plantation when William signed up for the war. He asked Daniel about signing up. Daniel said that he would sign up later. I believe he hesitated becasue he wanted to get to know me. William had to leave and he told Daniel to stay with mother and father for a while. Mother had been sick. Daniel was to help father with his work while father stayed closer to my mother. Daniel and I became close. We had many conversations. We took many walks together around the farm and rode our horses together. He looked so handsome in that saddle and was a brilliant rider. I remember the first time that he kissed me. We had been sitting in the den talking about his family and about William. He took my hand and held it. I still remember the warmth of his hand."sighing

"Daniel, I will call our cook for some refreshments," I said. I stood to go but he stood beside of me to stop me.

Daniel looked at me and said, "Marian, I do not have an appetite. My feelings are all about you. The first time that I laid eyes on you, I knew that you were the one for me. He pulled me close and we kissed. My heart felt faint and I could hardly stand. He had to hold me up. We sat back down on the sette' and just hugged one another.

The very next day, my father had heard that the war was getting closer. He asked Daniel to take me north to a safe place. The arrangements were made for Daniel to take me to New York to his mothe'rs home. Father prepared a carriage and provisions for us. I kissed my parents telling them that I would be back to see them soon. My father looked at me to say, I wish that were true. We all waved goodby and off we went. At first the travel was easy and we made headway. But about a week into traveling we started running into obstacles. We saw a few dead bodies along the road. Daniel became very alert and we started looking over our shoulders. I became a very good look-out while Daniel drove as cautiously as he could. Another day we heard shooting. Daniel drove our buggy into the trees to hide. The shooting was deafening. It was so close by that you could smell the gun powder, the smoke was so thick that you could not see very far ahead."

All of The Sewing Circle had stoped sewing and gave their full attention to Aunt Marian, even JoLynn joined them as hearing it all for the first time. Not much sewing was going on.

"Don't stop, what happened them," said Lorisa.

"Well, it was getting dark so we tied the horses to a tree and slept under the carriage. Daniel kept a lookout most of the night. I believe that he was afraid to fall asleep. I tried to relieve him a few hours so that he could get some sleep. The shooting finally stoped. Evidently they had moved on to another place. The next morning we traveled on. The road was clear for a long while. Then all of a sudden a union officer with several soldiers stoped our buggy. I was terrified inside. Daniel reasurred me that they were friendly. The officer talked to Daniel. He asked him where he was from and why he was out traveling. He was about to shoot him, I thought. I head the officer say."

"Young man, why are you not in uniform. There is a war going on. You are a traitor and you deserve to be shot." I was thinking that Daniel said that they were friendly. They did not seem friendly to me."

"Officer Whitley, Sir, I am a West Point graduate and as soon as I travel home I am signing up to join the war. I am traveling home now to sign up in my home state, New York. Then I will meet you on the battlefield."

The office looked at Daniel and said, "A West Pointer, hugh. That will make you an officer over me. When you join up, you will have a larger authority than I. I hope to see you when you become an officer. Until then have a safe trip, God speed."

"When Daniel drove off I could hear the relief in his breath. I also was very relieved. I have never been so scared. After that the roads were a little more clear until we ran across a bridge that had been demolished. We traveled a while down stream of the river until we saw a crossing. Danile got out of the buggy and led the two horses across the water. Finally we found the road and traveled on."

"I am so glad that the soldiers did not take our horses," said Daniel relieved.

"By that time I was calling him Danny Boy. He seemed to like the name and started calling me still, Marian. He said that he like that name because it sounded romantic to him. A few days later a wounded soldier came across our path. He tried to wave us down the best way that he could. He had no gun and he was bleeding from the left arm and leg. Daniel stopped to help him. He tore up one of his white shirts and bandaged up the soldier. He invited the soldier to join us in the buggy and he would try to find a doctor for him. The man said that the doctors were on the battlefield and he had to get back or he would be shot as a deserter. Daniel prayed over him and the soldier went back into the woods."

"We ran into a lot of debri on the road and had to stop several times to move it out of the way. I remember a small stream in Pennsylvania. We had stopped to camp for the night. We took turns taking a bath in the stream while we were also taking turns looking out for soldiers. It was all quiet. We had a bite to eat and began to feel relaxed. We were sitting beside the buggy on a blanket. Daniel said that he was sorry about all of the obstacles that we had encountered. I told him that it was not his fault. That I was glad that it was not any worse. I thanked him for my safey so far and looked forward to traveling on to meet his mother. He said, "Marian, you have been so brave. You are a trouper. When the war is over will you think about being my wife? I am not sure how long the war will last but I pray that it will be over soon. Many men from the north are still signing up to fight for our nation to be one and not be split up. I believe in the cause. Our nation needs to be a union. We will be stronger to be one. That is how it is in marriage. We will be stronger together. While I am on the battlefield, I will try harder to return knowing that you will be waiting for me. Think about it, take as long as you'd like before you answer me. I want you to be absolutely sure. Pray for me when I will be away."

"I already knew that I did not want this man to leave my side. But I did as he requested and waited a few days to give him an answer. We were almost running out of food. When we stopped for the evening, Daniel left for a few minutes and came back with a rabbit. He cleaned it and cooked it over the open fire. That rabbit was the first that I had ever eaten and so delicious. I knew that he would be a good provider. He thanked God for our provisions and our safety so far and for the safety to continue on. We finally made it to New York. That night before we reached his mother's home, I told Daniel how thankful I was for getting us safely through the war zone. Danny Boy, I said, I have been pondering your words about being your wife. I could have told you that day what was in my heart. But I am glad that you asked me to take time to think about your proposal. I definitely do want to be your wife. I started falling in love with you the day that we met. My love for you has grown deeper each day that we have been together. Let us not wait until after the war to get married. I want to be your wife as soon as possible. I feel that my prayers will be even deeper if you are my husband."

Daniel stopped the buggy and held my hands. "Marian you have made me the happiest man in all of God's creation. When we get to Mothers', we will tell her. Our pastor is a friend of the family and he will marry us. When I met his mother, Regina, I told her how very thankful I was to be residing in her home. Daniel and I got married the next day. A week later he signed up for the army. Regina and I saw him off from the train depot. Every day and every night I prayed for Daniel's safety. I had written my parents about making it safe to New York and about my marriage to Daniel. I still do not know if my parents ever received that letter. After the war, Daniel came home wounded. The wound healed in no time and he was back to normal. I nurtured him with all of my love and we had a marvelous life together. Our highlight as you all know, of course, was the birth of JoLynn. And now here we are almost forty years later after the war. It has been a long life but yet such a short one. When Danny Boy died in the railroad accident, I wanted to die with him. God has a way to keep us going. I am enjoying Annette. My heart has mostly healed and I look forward to seeing my family mature. And now I have all of you."

"Aunt Marian that was so romantic, just like I imagioned it except better. Thank you for telling us," said Lorisa.

"Aunt Marian, you should write a book. I am keeping a journal and I will include your story along with ours," said Abby.

"A journal, then you will have the family history written down. I will just have to read it sometime," said Aunt Marian.

Everyone commented about the story and Aunt Marian was happy to share.

15

It was Christmas and everyone was excited. They all commented on the wonderful dinner and settled in to the living room for the children to open their presents. The family just kept growing. Carlos, Teresa, Jose, and Rachel had made moccasins for all of the children including Annette. The children put on their shoes and wore them around the house. It as a good thing that Rae had a very large ranch house. Lorisa played the piano and everyone gathered around to sing their favorite Christmas carols. Rae commented about the ten pointed star on top of the Christmas tree to remembering their brother Billy and everyone said cheers. The siblings could still feel the loneliness of missing Billy. Rae said that when Billy was thrown from the horse and found dead that everyone was devastated. It took a long time to heal. But they all worked together about the situation. They told Aunt Marian and cousin JoLynn about his story, then they all gathered around holding hands and Rae said a prayer.

"I keep hearing bits and pieces about my brother. I am glad that he was a good father to you all. I especially admire him for his love for Angelina. I am sorry that he was away so much. Why did he just not move you all closer to his job. Did Angelina not want to leave Mexico? I feel as though that I need to know. Why did he just not take you all closer to his work instead of traveling back and forth so much. He was a great provider; making sure that you all were cared for and leaving you a legacy."

"Aunt Marian, I will tell you the story the best that I know how," said Rae. "You deserve to know the truth and I know more than anyone else since I am the oldest. We loved our father very much. He meant the world to us. After seeing his and your home burned down after the war with carpetbaggers and scalawags squating on the farm, there was nothing that he could do. He was outraged about what had happened. He vowed to get his rightful ownership back, but he was not sure how to do that. When he met two other men in the same delima, all being betrayed by the war, they all decided to get some of their money back from the ones that had stolen it all. That is what they thought at the time. The three men formed a gang and robbed stage coaches and banks. Father was thinking that he was justifying himself. I did not know about this until I saw a wanted picture in Lizzy's father's office. He is our, Sheriff Wade Ward. Father went to Mexico to hide out from the law and bounty hunters. There he met our mother, Angelina Salinas.

After we had become young adults, we decided to leave Mexico and come to the states. We did not get very far. We were still very young. Billy was only about six years old at the time. I was eighteen and knew that we all could work it out together. Father had taught me well about handling money and being a good business man. I had saved some money from our father's treasure and we stopped here in Austin. I got a job working with Wells Fargo Bank and later bought this ranch. It has been remolded several times to keep up with modern conveniences. Father returned to us a few years before he died. He had met a circuit rider preacher on the range one day and father accepted the Lord as his personal Savior. He came to us asking forgiveness. We asked him live in the house with us but he said that he did not want to embarrass us. He asked Ryon and me to hire him as a ranch hand and he would stay in the bunk house. We pleaded with him but he would have it any other way. After he had been with us a few years, Ryon found him on the ground in the barn, he was dead clutching the wooden cross that he had given our mother as a gift, to his chest.

When we first arrived at our ranch we all named it The Circle Cross Ranch after the love of the cross from our parents. He was a good man. He just got turned around in his way of thinking about his vindication. He is buried behind the house on the small hill over looking the stream beside of our brother Billy."

"I almost wish that I had not asked," said Aunt Marian. He always was a little head strong. But the past is the past. Thank God that he realized his mistake and turned to our Savior. That is the most important part and we will see him in heaven along with our other family members. One day we will all be together again. That is something to look forward to. We all make mistakes. Thank God for His forgiving mercies and grace."

"There is just one more story and I do not want to leave it out. A few months after Danny Boy came home, as we were retiring for the night, Danny told me that in the last battle he ran across William lying on the ground bleeding. When Danny saw him, he dismounted his horse and ran over to William. No one was watching him because the battle was so intense. If someone did see him they might would have thought that he was checking to see if the soldier was dead. Danny tore his own shirt and wrapped up William's wound to stop the bleeding. He said a prayer over William and prayed that the doctors would find him alive. William was going in and out of conciousness. William recognized him and told Daniel, thank you. We both cried that night and said a prayer for William."

"Just think," said Ryon. If it had not been for Daniel saving our father none of us would be here today. Now Daniel is my hero also."

"Aunt Marian, thank God that we met you. Daniel is a hero to this whole family. I am so glad to hear all of the stories. We will continue on with them each day. You are right, this story can not be told in a day," said Abby.

"Thursday, we will all go over to Ryon's to have a cook out. My mouth is watering for those t-bone steaks. He also has Porterhouse and filet mignon, whatever you want. You can put your order in now. I want the jucy t-bone, medium rare," said Rae.

16

Rae walked into the kitchen to see Aunt Jame and Uncle Eli. He saw Ryon's cooks talking with them. "Howdy," said Rae. "What brings you two to our kitchen? Are your all comparing recipes?"

"Actually we are", Janice said. "Aunt Jame and Uncle Eli and Henry and I are swapping recipes. We do not want them to get lost. We are writing a cook book. Everyone needs to know about these wonderful recipes."

"Remember Rae that I told you that our recipes were never given out. Now is the time to get them into the public's hands. We want everyone to enjoy our recipes."

"That is a good idea. I do want to share. I would hate to hog them all to myself."

"Rae this will take a little while, Aunt Jame and Uncle Eli are demonstrating the making of their recipes. That way I can write them all down in detail and make sure all of the ingredients are perfect," said Janice. "Once they are printed, we all may even sell our recipe books at the merchantile store."

"We all are making desserts for the big cook out at Ryon's this Thursday, said Janice. "I know that you, Ryon, and John are cooking the steaks but we will make everything else. Henry and I are looking forward to this big shing dig."

"We are doing a lot of cooking Rae. We will be distributing food to all of the families. You all will be our samplers. It is good that we have guests. They will return home with full stomachs," said Uncle Eli.

"We all have full stomachs thanks to your cooking. I am ready to sample anything that you all come up with. Just give me a holler," said Rae. Rae snatched a sample of an apple turnover and walked out of the door with a big bite and saying, "aaaugh."

"Well,l believe that receipe for the apple turnovers passes," said Henry.

17

Everyone was at Ryon's cook out. Rae and Lizzy were there with their children Willy and Lilly. D'Anna and John with Matthew, Luke, and Angie. There was Abby and Mark with Charles and Cindy. Then of course there was Ryon and Claire with their children Theresa and Ryon Junior. Lorisa and Lesley with their children Billy and Paul. That is the immediate Jefferson family for now. Lydia and Pastor Joe with Luke, Nancy, Joe Junior, and Grace were there. Then of course their were Aunt Marian and her daughter JoLynn with her daughter Annette. It was just one of those special family reunions. The children played, the mothers took care of the younger ones, and the men pitched in to cook the steaks and help with the food that Henry and Janice had prepared.

It was all over too soon. Everyone was enjoying themselves. Aunt Marian, cousin JoLynn and second cousin Annetter were leaving next week.

"This has been a pleasure. What a delightful family. I have been missing a lot, but I plan to be included more in the future. JoLynn and I were talking the other night. We both decided to sell my home in Pennsylvania and I will move in with them in mother's house in New York. The house is historical and we want to preserve it," said Aunt Marian.

"It will be good for you all to be together. You will be there for Annette's adult years and I know that you do not want to miss that," said Abby. "It is good for family to be together. Our family enjoys beging together. Now if we can just get Lorisa to live closer."

"I will be closer than you think. With the new cars arriving soon it will only take us a day instead of two days to get here. So I am already closer. Lesley and I will just whizz by."

"Okay, before you all leave, Aunt Marian, all of us will have a picnic next Tuesday down by the lake, said John. "D'Anna and I have it all planned out."

"We enjoyed discussing all the things that we will do. Wear play clothes because we all may get a little dirt and water on us. Guys, you all bring your fishing poles. I have already talked with the ladies and we have planned to make picnic baskets with lots of food," said D'Anna.

"My family is spoiling me rotten. I will never get over this. What a delightful time that I am having and I'm sure that I am speaking for JoLynn and Annette also", said Aunt Marian.

"Mother, I can surely speak for myself on this matter. This is the best vacation that I have ever attended. I call it a vacation because I am enjoying it so much. I look forward to the next Christmas family reunion. It will be hard to leave to go back home. Mother and I have a lot to discuss about the house and moving arrangements and I would appreciate all of your prayers."

"You all are definitely in our prayers," said Lizzy. "I know that we all will be praying for you both to make the right decisions. We pray that all works out well. I am sure that it will."

After the meal and everyone was leaving to go home, the leftover food was distributed out to the ranch hands and they had their own feast.

18

On the way back to Rae's ranch, Aunt Marian said, "Rae you have been such a good provider to all of your family. You are a very sharing and giving person. I really do admire you and all of your siblings. Ryon is very intelligent in his business. D'Anna, Abby, and Lorisa are wonderful Christian ladies. They make their home a pleasure to live in. Your parents must have been very loving and kind. I see this in all of you. It makes me proud to be William's sister. He had to do something good for you all to turn out the way that you are. I love each one of you dearly. My heart just sings with the joy of the Jefferson family."

"I also saw that in Rae and his family. That is one reason that I married him. He still is deligent in his integrity. You don't find many families like the Jefferson family."

"I do not take any credit whatsoever. I trust and obey God to do the right things," said Rae.

"I am happy to hear that," said Aunt Marian. "Only if everyone would see life in that manner, it would be a better world."

"Now have I heard everything about my brother. Or is there still a serect no one has mentioned."

"Aunt Marian, even though father was considered an outlaw, he was the best father that I could have imagined. He showed his love for his family and he provided well for us. He was a giver. At the end he helped people meet their needs. He became a missionary here at the ranch. He preached the gospel to the ranch hands that lived in the bunk house. I heard that several fellows got saved. Father preached that the only way to heaven was through Jesus Christ, God's son even though Jesus is God Himself. God came to give His all so that we could be reconiled to Him. We all miss father and his legacy to man."

"I heard him tell some fellows, when they could not understand how a son could be the father too."

He said, "just imagion the egg. It has three parts. The three parts make it a whole egg. It is still just one egg. One egg with three parts. The Father, the Son, and the Holy Spirit. Does that help in your understanding?"

"I heard a ranch hand say."

"it does make more sense now. Thank you William for sharing that with us, helping us to understand."

"We all have three parts to us. We have the body as you can see, we have our soul, and we have a spirit. It all relates back to the trinity. Father sent them all over to Pastor Joe Hodges and he baptised them in the creek."

19

It was Tuesday, time for the big event picnic. The great visit was winding down, coming to an end. The picnic was so enjoyable but a little sad too because Aunt Marian, JoLynn, and Annette were leaving to go home the next day. The picnic tables were filled with delicious food. The ladies gathered around to talk while the men threw out their fishing lines into the lake.

"Aunt Marian, it is hard to say goodby. We all will miss you, JoLynn, and Annette terribly. Lesley and I are staying another day and then we will be traveling home. We will correspond often and keep up with each other," said Lorisa.

"I will be writing many letters. I want to know all about the families and the children. You all must come to visit us in New York when you can. Our home has extra bedrooms and are very cozy," said Aunt Marian.

"Now that we know that you are here, let us not be strangers," said D'Anna. "I will be glad to fill you in on all of our events."

"I will need another journal," said Abby. "My second journal is about filled already. Now I can include you three. Keep the letters coming and I will write all of the events into my journal."

"Abby, I throughly enjoyed you having all of us ladies at your house the other day for tea. It has been a long time since I was invited to a tea. We used to have them all the time when I was a little girl. It brought back many memories. Please add that to your journal," said Aunt Marian.

The guys had caught enough fish for the whole family. They cleaned the fish and cooked them over the open coals of the fire. The sun was setting and cast a golden and red haze over the camp. Everyone marveled at the sight.

"We need to pack up so that we can make it safely home," said Rae. "This has been a great day, I surely have enjoyed it."

"Aunt Marian, I will say goodby now because you will be leaving early in the morning and we will not see you again for a while," said Ryon. Ryon and Claire and their family said their goodbys and hitched up their buggy to go home.

Mark and Abby said goodby and left with their family. D'Anna and John and their family said goodby, gathered up their children and rode home.

Lesley and Lorisa gathered up the remains of the picinic baskets and headed back to Rae's house with their family, following Rae and Lizzy with their children.

Aunt Marian, JoLynn, Annette, Williy, Lilly, Lizzy, and Rae rode back home together. Everyone was tired from the day and settled down for the night.

The next morning Lorisa got up early to say goodby to Aunt Marian. "Aunt Marian, it has been a pleasure having you here." She hugged her, JoLynn, and Annette and said goodby.

Rae and Lizzy drove the three guests to the train depot. "Please come again as soon as you all can. Our home is always open to you. We look forward to seeing you again," said Lizzy.

"Thank you Lizzy. Thank you Rae for being a perfect host and hostess. We need to get back to take care of all of our business and make decisions about moving. It has been absolutely wonderful to have been here with you all. We must board now. Hope to see you all in the near future. Goodby," said Aunt Marian.

"Goodby," said JoLynn and Annette together.

Rae walked with them closer to the train entrance and hugged them all. "Thank you for coming. I am praying for your safe trip back home. Write often."

They all said goodby again as Rae and Lizzy watched the train leave. On the way home they talked about another great adventure for their memories.

20

When Gloria became pregnant, Ross was estatic. He made sure that she had the best of everything. "Ross, I am only having a baby. I can still work and do things for myself. I will let you know if I need anything special. During the meantime, just relax and enjoy this beautiful time together." Ross would feel of her stomach every day. "I am anxious to feel it kick. Does the pregency feel like a boy or a girl?" asked Ross.

"Well you can not always tell but by the way that I am carrying her. She is different than carrying Bobby. I believe that she is a girl."

"Oh, I do hope so. It really doesn't matter but I have always wanted a little girl," said Ross. "I see all these little girls come in at the store and they look so pretty in their dresses and they are so delicate. I would give her the moon if I could. What are we going to name her, presuming it is a girl?"

"Why don't you name her, Ross. You always have good names for the specialties that we sell in the store."

"I have been thinking about a name. I want both of us to agree on her name. I kinda like the name Julia. I do not know anyone with that name. How does Julia sound?"

"Julia is a pretty name. I like it. Julia Marie it is."

"Yes, Julia Marie Russell, doesn't that sound precious," said Ross. "She will be so very special."

"Don't be silly, Ross. She will be like any other girl. Just love her and help her to mature in a Godly fashion. Each person has his or her own personality and they have to make their own choices once they mature. We will work together to give her the right atmosphere."

"She will be special to our family. I will be happy to accept a boy as well as a girl. I was just talking," said Ross.

When the time came for Gloria to have her baby, Ross ran to get the doctor. The doctor was not in his office so he ran over to Lydia's. "Lydia please hurry, Gloria is about to give birth. I heard that you are a midwife and I surely do need your help."

"I am coming. Just let me get Luke and Nancy to take care of Grace and Joe Jr. I will grab my birthing bag. Luke, tell your father where I am when he comes home."

Lydia helped Gloria deliver a beautiful baby girl. Gloria was doing fine. Ross was walking back and forth in the living room of their apartment. When he heard his daughter cry, he cried himself. Ross and Bobby walked to the bedroom door at the same time.

"You both can come in now and see Julia Marie," said Lydia.

Gloira was holding the baby in her arms when Ross and Bobby walked in. "Oh, mom, she is so beautiful. I am proud to have a baby sister. But don't ask me to change any diapers," said Bobby.

Ross just stood there. He was frozen to the floor. He could not believe that he had a baby girl. He was grinning from ear to ear. All he could think of to say was, "Oh God, thank you for this wonderful moment in time. Help me to be the father that You mean for me to be." He walked over to Gloria and she place the baby in her daddy's arms.

A few weeks later The Sewing Circle visited and gave many baby clothes to Gloria. Some were new and some had been handed down from their own families.

A month later, Pastor Hodges had a baby dedication for all of the babies that had been born in the past year. He asked the parents, "Do you promise to teach these babies as they mature to grow up in the Lord. To nurture them in God's Biblical Word? Church do you promise to help with the upbringing of these babies and help teach them the true and living Word?"

The church all promised to help with the maturing of the children to serve the Lord. It as a good service. One to remember and cherish.

Printed in the United States
By Bookmasters